NORTHERN IRELAND

Photographs by
Robert Blair & Bill Kirk

Text by
Ian Hill

THE
BLACKSTAFF PRESS
BELFAST

First published in 1986 by
The Blackstaff Press Limited
3 Galway Park, Dundonald, Belfast BT16 0AN, Northern Ireland
with the assistance of the
Industrial Development Board
of Northern Ireland

Reprinted 1988, 1991, 1994

Printed in England by
BAS Printers Limited

British Library Cataloguing in Publication Data
Blair, Robert, 1943–
Northern Ireland.
1. Photography – Landscapes   2. Travel
photography – Northern Ireland   3. Northern
Ireland – Description and travel – 1981–
– Views
I. Title   II. Kirk, Bill   III. Hill, Ian,
1937–
779'.36'09416   TR660

Library of Congress Cataloging-in-Publication Data
Blair, Robert, 1943–
Northern Ireland.
1. Northern Ireland – Description and travel –
1981–   – Views.   I. Kirk, Bill.   II. Hill, Ian,
1937–   III. Title.
DA990.U45B49   1986   914.1604824   86-8296
ISBN 0-85640-365-2

CONTENTS

NORTHERN IRELAND

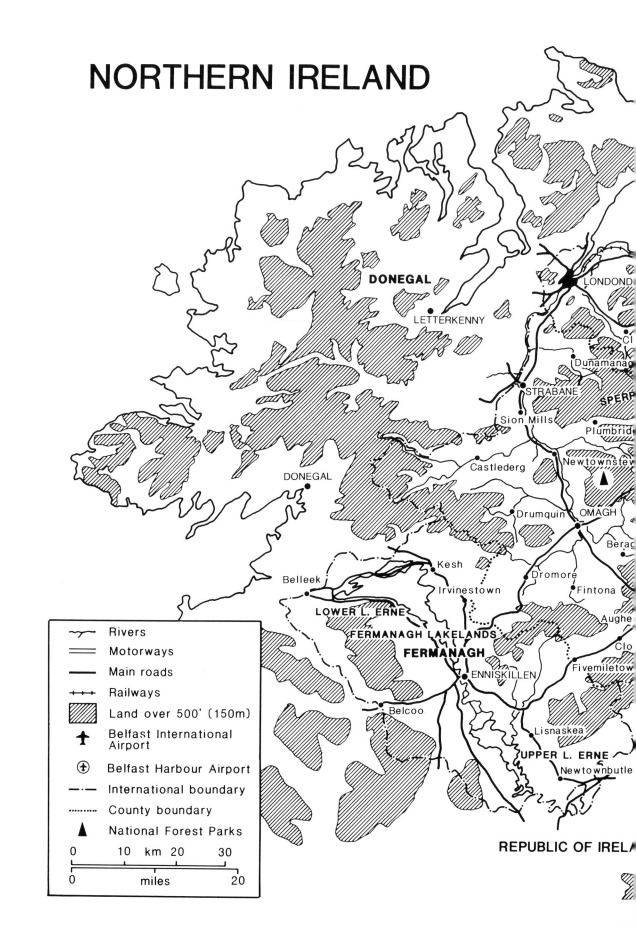

DONEGAL

LETTERKENNY

LONDOND

CI

Dunamanag

STRABANE

SPERR

Sion Mills

Plumbrid

Castlederg

Newtownstev

DONEGAL

▲

Drumquin

OMAGH

Berag

Kesh

Dromore

Fintona

Belleek

Irvinestown

LOWER L. ERNE

Aughe

FERMANAGH LAKELANDS

Clo

FERMANAGH

Fivemiletow

ENNISKILLEN

Belcoo

Lisnaskea

UPPER L. ERNE

Newtownbutle

REPUBLIC OF IRELA

Legend

〰	Rivers
≡	Motorways
—	Main roads
+++	Railways
▨	Land over 500' (150m)
✈	Belfast International Airport
⊕	Belfast Harbour Airport
—·—·—	International boundary
········	County boundary
▲	National Forest Parks

```
0      10   km  20      30
0              miles        20
```

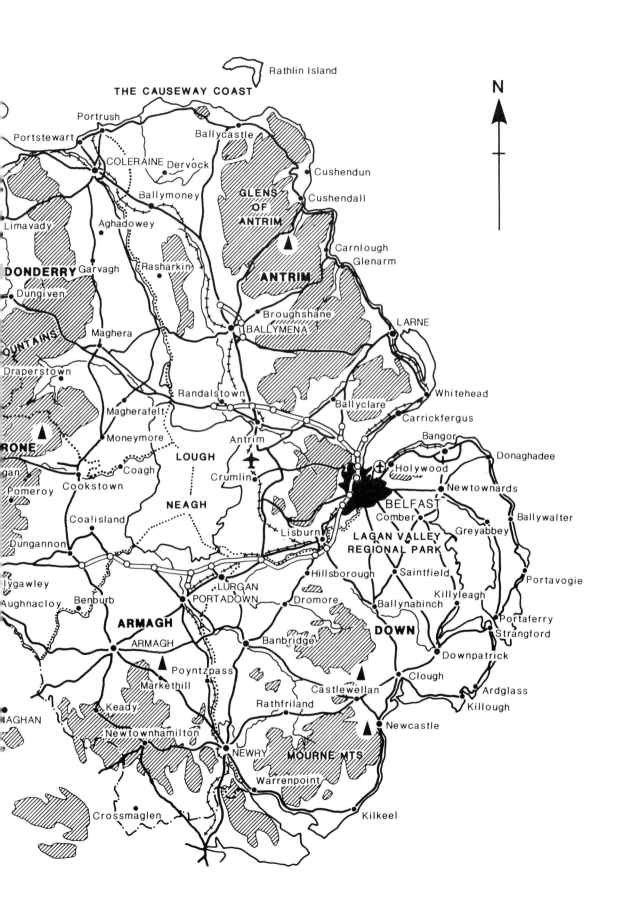

INTRODUCTION

A book falls open at your favourite pages. So do countries. Try as you will, it is difficult not to go back to the same town, the same street, the same bar. And so this book of images is a book of favourites.

The winding streets of hilly Ulster towns, the Diamonds where the hilly streets meet, the statues to the fallen at the Somme are all part of the vernacular of the architecture, along with home bakeries, finest wines and spirit importers and gothic-revival Church of Ireland churches. The villages, cheerful in their neglect by the motorway and the dual carriageway, glimpsed only, by some, as a spiked spire between distant breast-like drumlins. The fairy-rings of hill forts, now circled with beech-trees, are tantalising if glimpsed from a passing car, and marvellous in their symmetry if viewed coming in to land by plane. Or sailing up Belfast Lough on a summer evening, the city glowing gold in its gentle saucer of hills, the hills themselves painted backdrops to the tiny canyons of the dusty streets.

The cities, all pubs and churches, betting shops and banks, the corner shops and the Art Deco cinemas gone to Chinese take-aways and video clubs, though in the city-villages, between centre and suburb, not all Medical Halls have become pharmacies, not all hardware stores taken their new spades in off the pavement. In the early morning Belfastmen walk greyhounds up into the hills for exercise and if they ever look back they will see the lough coming out of the mist beside the great cranes of the shipyard.

Further round the coast are the noisy pleasures of gulls' squabbles when the fleets come back to tiny coastal harbours, or the sight of distant tractors edging like mechanical spiders across the rich Co. Down hills. Harvesters working in the setting sun in Antrim and Derry fields, their view west, white horses on a blue sea, a scatter of boats, and then, if they want to imagine it, America.

On early seaside mornings when you can't sleep the sharp light creeps along the stucco of the Victorian villas, each turned to small hotel or bed-and-breakfast. Before the first ice cream of the day, savour their ice-cream colours. . . pistachio, strawberry, vanilla, coffee, banana. A milkman's float passes, the milkman waving. A boy goes from door to door delivering the *News Letter* and the *Irish News*, but never, in this place of hard-edged politics, both through the same letterbox.

The lush lakes of Fermanagh, the water warm-brown with turf from the mountains, its edge spiked with reed mace and flag iris. Tiny flies over a cow's head as it ruminates, hock deep in the lapping lake. The curl of other flies as the trout fisherman's line catches the May sun in its looping curve.

Still avenues of heavy silences between the dark brown-green tented acres of spruce and fir in the forest parks. Standing stones in a farmer's yard, another in his front garden, a ring of them across the ditch of yellow prickly gorse. The Sperrin Mountains all about you.

And the most abiding image, completely unphotographable, yet once encountered never forgotten. It's 'crack' and it has never been defined. In part it is all those images just described – to which have been added the personality of the people. . . engaging, confiding, suspicious, welcoming, inquisitive, ironic in turns. Fond of their pubs and their churches in almost equal amounts. Rarely trying to pretend that the current 'troubles' have not had their effects but insisting that these should not be exaggerated. Travelling about, you cannot avoid seeing the material damage that both the town-planner and the inter-necine conflict have wrought, mostly confined to a few towns. All the rest, they will tell you – and truly – is unspoilt countryside and undisturbed and beautiful coastline.

Aird's Snout (opposite)

The
CAUSEWAY COAST

The Giant's Causeway: the Chimneys

October 1588. Don Alonzo Martinez, Senor de la Casa de Levia de Rioja was on the run. Crammed with 1,300 men into the galleass *Girona*, he was making for home. The Armada was defeated and the clumsy, overloaded galleas wasn't the ship to be on in an Atlantic storm. Mistaking the Chimneys of the Giant's Causeway for those of Dunluce Castle, where Sorley Boy MacDonnell might be expected to give him shelter, he ran the *Girona* aground at what became known as Port na Spaniagh.

Salmon fishermen, Ballintoy

Only nine men survived the *Girona,* and for almost four hundred years it lay on the sea bottom, eluding treasure hunters. But as a result of its rediscovery in 1967 the *Girona's* ducats, muskets, jewelled chains, golden cameos and even inkwells can now be seen in the Ulster Museum, Belfast. These salmon fishermen and their ancestors have concentrated on plucking a different sort of treasure from the sea.

The harbour, Ballintoy

The first Ballintoy harbour was built by an eighteenth-century confidence trickster by the name of 'Graceless' Stewart to facilitate the shipping of the poor local coal to Dublin; he received a huge government grant for his efforts. Well above the harbour stands a tiny church where Protestants took refuge during the 1641 rebellion; they were kept alive by the local Catholic priest who smuggled in oatmeal in their waterbuckets. The harbour makes a splendid embarcation point for a sea tour of the Chimneys, Aird's Snout, the Priest and his Flock and the other strange volcanic formations in the Giant's Causeway, reputedly built in a fury by the Irish giant Finn MacCool, spoiling for fisticuffs with his rival in Scotland.

Bushmills

Bushmills in the sunshine. Bask in the main square, or walk the neat narrow streets, buying feathers and lures to catch cod and haddock, plaice and mackerel, pink pouting, and grunting grey gurnard out of Portballintrae. Buy a needle, or a haystack. Listen to the dark brown rush of river Bush water under the bridge, round the island, past the old mill race. Smell turf smoke in the crisp air.

But come back in the winter. Come in off the wet streets where the wind plucks at your clothes and ripples tiny pavement puddles. Red-fingered, order a 'hot Bush' and watch the old lady behind the bar warm the glass from a kettle and toss away the water. She adds brown sugar, cloves, a pinch of cinnamon. A measure of 'Black Bush', topped with hot water. Then you can welcome winter, sipping one of the four products of the oldest licensed distillery in the world.

Dunluce Castle (right)

4

Rathlin Island

You could go to Rathlin just because it's there. Or to scuba-dive in the sharp blueness of the sun-sparkled sea. Or to fish for trout in the reed-fringed waters of the tiny lakes. You could pad the loose stone loneys to the wind-carved volcanic stacks and try to count the June shearwaters, fulmars, kittiwakes, razorbills, guillemots and posing puffins on the guano-white ledges. Seek Robert the Bruce's cave. Search for flakes of flint at Brockley, for Rathlin porcellanite axes were the designer weapons of the Stone Age. Ponder on celibacy, if you must, in the eighth-century monastic sweat house at Knockans. Or you could just lie in the flowery meadows. Hear the skylark. Spy the buzzard. Read Michael McLaverty's marvellous stories about island life.

Carrick-a-Rede Rope Bridge

Whitepark Bay is so beautiful, it makes you smile. Children, a moment ago tired, sweaty and car-sick, whoop across the boundless sand. Lovers lie amongst meadow cranesbill and vernal squill watching Holly Blues flutter by. By the water's edge, old men's white legs stand revealed by rolled-up trousers. Bunioned toes rake for top shells and cowries, mermaid's purses and gulls' skulls.

Geologists poke at the dark blue lias clay for fossils, and belemnites nudge out of the chalk cliffs. Mesolithic flints lie just beneath the sand hills' shifting slopes, and up the hill behind Ballintoy rectory there is a 'giant's grave', a megalithic tomb.

Portbraddan, a cluster of white houses, one of them the smallest church in Ireland, clings improbably to the rocks. And there's the rope bridge at Carrick-a-Rede, slung up in the summer by commercial salmon fishermen getting to their nets.

**Salmon fishermen at
Carrick-a-Rede (left)**

7

Kinbane Castle (left)

Bonamargy Friary (above)

Have a look at Kinbane (*ceann bán* – the white head) Castle from the B15, or put the car in the carpark and explore – but cautiously! Grace Staple's cave is hereabouts, but it, like the ruins of the gatehouse turrets at Kinbane, may be considered less than safe for the casual Sunday driver. A MacDonnell built Kinbane, like so much else around here. That was in 1547 and just four years later it was taken by the English troops. MacDonnell took it back again. Of course.

Drive the dipping, curling road round this coast. Each headland carries a crumbling castle: Sorley Boy MacDonnell and his descendants were hard men in hard times. Men who understood the power of terror, and who knew that a strong castle to a warrior was as a cave to a sleeping bear. At Bonamargy Friary, east of Ballycastle, at the mouth of the Margy river, they say the grass never grew in the graveyard. It never had time to. It was constantly being dug up to make way for fresh graves. Not wanting to be disturbed in so peremptory a fashion, Sorley Boy had his massive coffin locked in a vault. The caretaker has the key though.

The Diamond, Ballycastle

Ballycastle is too nice a town to call confusing – but it is. There is Ballycastle the port, and there is Ballycastle the market town crouched snugly in hilly streets running gently to the Diamond. Tennis players volley and McEnroe on courts built over by the harbour, on summer Sundays queues form at the ice-cream parlours, and farmers, treble-parked in rust-bitten Fords, spare no thought for the traveller's revving Renault as they mourn the coming harvest.

Ould Lammas Fair (opposite)

The pubs are full. Beer cans and stout bottles fringe the Marconi memorial. On top of Knocklayde mountain, which towers over the tiny revelling town, farmboys doze fitfully by the prehistoric cairn. The boat plies to and fro from Rathlin Island. Old men with strong hard chins match fiddle tunes with sandal-wearers left behind from the Sixties. Handlers trot hairy ponies on street and pavement and carpetbaggers with accents ranging from Pakistan to Putney promise endless purchases on offer at less than cost. In fact they are thinking of paying us to take the goods away.

Fair Head

In the summer you can think back to the Causeway and that ebullient giant Finn MacCool. But winter at Fair Head is the province of the Grey Man, more massive than the Kraken, rising from the deep, the swirl of his cape darkening the whole sky, the casual cruel brush of his ankle spilling five-thousand-ton basalt columns onto the sea shore. A monstrous fissure marks the Grey Man's path. Wild goats prance in his tracks. A single clap of his hands blew the *Girona* onto the rocks. Across the sea of Moyle, past the Slough-na-Morra whirlpool, the Children of Lir were turned to swans for an eternity.

The Ould Lammas Fair, Ballycastle

A plaque on a wall in Ann Street asks, in memory of songwriter John McAuley:

Did you treat your Mary Ann
To dulse and yellow man
At the ould Lammas Fair at
Ballycastle – O?

Dulse is iodine-rich chewing seaweed, Yellow Man is chewing toffee. Once a harvest-time hiring-fair for Ballycastle, Rathlin, the Glens of Antrim, and for the canny folk of the west coast of Scotland, the Lammas Fair is today what you make of it. Fun fair and children's outing, meat teas and frying-steak, bottles of stout opened in the open air, buskers hustling, hustlers busking, shore-fishing from the Salt Pans.

Shepherd on the Antrim coast

Waterfall in Glenariff (opposite)

The
GLENS

The river Dun and its viaduct

Wind whistles over the trackless acres of the Antrim plateau. Cut turf-banks and wavering white bog-cotton, a hooded crow pecking at unseen carrion, a sparrow-hawk hovering for grouse chicks in the heather. But in the cleavage of the glens whose little rivers drain the harsh moorlands, men nestle in comforting warmth. Inevitably, in their isolation, the people of the tiny villages cling to and treasure a past which is indeed past. Village shops carry slim volumes by local authors, anecdotal, spiked with fairytales and ghosts. But these are comforting fairies. There is little want here of the terrors of the deep. If your cousin to the north has to live in fear of the Grey Man's second coming, let him.

Glentaisie, the glen of the princess Taisie, and Glenshesk, the glen of the sedges, run south to north, down to Ballycastle. Glendun, the brown glen, runs north-east into the sea at Cushendun. Glencorp, the glen of the slaughter, runs into Glendun from the south. Glenann, the steepsided glen, and Glenballyeamon, Edward's glen and town, meet the sea at Cushendall. Glenariff, the ploughman's glen, runs down to Waterfoot and Red Bay. Glencloy, glen of the hedges, debouches at Carnlough, and Glenarm, glen of the army, at Glenarm village.

The river Dun (opposite)

On a summer's evening cars parked bumper deep in the long grass on the meadows or meadow sweet verges of the narrow lanes are the first sign. Stop yours, wind down the window and like as not, amongst the sweetness of the flowers you'll catch the fuller complementary smell of Murray's Erinmore. You're on to your first trout fisherman of the day. Tread softly or you'll tread on his dreams of brown trout gasping in the riverbank sedges. Or better still a salmon.

There are salmon to be caught in the Margy, the Carey, the Shesk, the Dun, the Dall and the Glen. At night a car at the verge could be a poacher. Drive on, dreamer.

Jim McKillop's violin (left)

Well, it was Jim McKillop's then. It will be sold by now, for Jim, who lives in Carnlough, makes the best of fiddles. Each county in Ireland has a fiddling style of its own and the pubs around the Glens are easy places to hear good Antrim fiddling. This isn't the music of the hairy beer-bellied Aran-sweatered gang; Glens musicians are playing for their own and their peers' delight.

Knocklayde and Ballycastle Forest (left)

Up the airy mountain,
Down the rushy glen,
We daren't go a-hunting,
For fear of little men.

And yet, and yet. . . for Antrim men were amongst those who were the frontiersmen in the new west, in the Americas. Theodore Roosevelt, whose mother's family came from County Antrim, wrote of them: 'They were a grim, stern people, strong and simple, powerful for good and evil. . . relentless, revengeful, suspicious, knowing neither ruth nor pity. . . they were of all men the best fitted to conquer the wilderness and hold it against all comers.' The families of Presidents Jackson, Johnson, Arthur, Cleveland and McKinley were also Antrim folk.

Carnlough

Ulster's vernacular architecture leads itself into eccentric cul-de-sacs, so catch them now before the country runs awash with bungalows and haciendas. In Carnlough the main street is dominated by a limestone bridge which spans the roadway and a Georgian coaching inn.

The bridge dates from 1854 when it was constructed to carry a narrow gauge railway from limestone quarries in the hills, down to the limestone harbour. Nowadays the harbour is a mooring place for private yachts, a few lobster boats and ocean-going yachts seeking a last haven on their chancy way to the Western Isles.

Glenarm

Anne Katherine MacDonnell became Countess of Antrim in her own right in 1791 and married a Mr Phelps, a chorister of Wells Cathedral. Phelps, obviously not a Glensman, made her promise to give up the drink and settle down and build a decent castle and certainly one with a decent gateway to impress callers. We can ponder on Mr Phelps attractions, for, whatever they were, the gothic barbican gate archway at the entrance of the Antrim estates was one of their results. The family, which picked the wrong side once or twice in history, survived through the female line, and like everyone else with power on this fractious coast derives from old Sorley Boy MacDonnell himself. If the chalk dust isn't too thick, walk the village and note the curious street names. William Makepeace Thackeray liked them too.

The view from Lurigethan (right)

Lych-gate, Broughshane (right)

Up the Glenarm valley, past The Sheddings and down into the valley of the Braid with Slemish mountain on your left and you come to Broughshane and the canny people on the fringes of Ballymena. The lych-gate is an unexpected frivolity here in a town which produced the ancestors of Sam Houston, hero of the Alamo, and General Sir George White, VC, hero of Ladysmith.

But before you leave the Glens you must collect some further architectural delights. You've seen Charles Lanyon's viaduct over the Dun river, but you should go on down into Cushendun to see what Clough Williams Ellis, a man who built a curiosity when he could, made of this delightful estuarial village.

Snow near Slemish (below)

Gateposts near Slemish

At breakfast the farmer's daughter took the order and called to the kitchen for two 'fries', one for a gentleman, the other for the lady. The white linen tablecloth disappeared beneath the plates of wheaten bread, soda bread, hot toast, freshly rolled pats of butter and pots of home-made jam, raspberry, strawberry and damson. A great silver tea pot radiated heat in the centre.

The mystery of how you sex 'fries' was solved. By the eggs. A gentleman's had two, a lady's one. Apart from the eggs, the plate spilled over with two rashers of bacon, a couple of sausages, two pieces of potato bread, a slice of soda bread, all fried, and some mysterious susbtances, which upon enquiry, brought a slight blush to the already rosy cheeks of the farmer's daughter. She explained they were '. . .

bull's. . . well. . . testicles'. Not every Ulster breakfast is as overpowering as this but you'll find that many fall not far short of it. The province is still mainly rural and the tradition of a good breakfast for the working man dies hard. With one of those inside you you may not need lunch so the news that many Ulster people don't have any may not disturb you. They do, however, eat dinner.

But that's an evening meal, you say, and you're partly right. An explanation: in hotels you'll find the usual regime of breakfast, lunch and dinner. But in slightly less sophisticated establishments – and in these north-eastern counties of the island there are still one or two which describe themselves simply as 'eating houses' – it may be breakfast, dinner and high tea.

Dinner (lunch to you) may be an Irish stew of just lamb, leeks, carrots, potatoes and lots of salt (and some

people consider the carrot an unnecessary frippery), or boiled Ballymoney ham with cabbage, onions and a simple white sauce. This can be washed down, if you're lucky, with buttermilk.

After 'dinner' at lunch-time, you might just feel peckish before 'high tea' at dinner-time. You can always drop in somewhere for afternoon tea; a big pot of strong tea and half a dozen kinds of bread and scones. There's soda bread, made on a griddle from baking soda, flour, salt, sugar and more buttermilk; wheaten bread, apple soda and currant bread; and beautiful barmbrack, a yeast bread full of currants which should be toasted in front of an open fire and smothered in butter.

And high tea? Well, that's a bit like breakfast all over again, with a chop thrown in, and another five or six kinds of bread and three or four varieties of home-made jams.

Slemish Mountain

Miluic, who ran things at Slemish in the fifth century, believed in the old gods of wrath and retribution. He wasn't a very nice person and gave Saint Patrick a grim time when he bought him as a slave to herd swine on these slopes. Patrick, wily lad, escaped, but when Miluic heard he was returning as a missionary in AD 423 he committed suicide. Understandably, for why should the wrath of a new unknown god be any less than that of the known?

Portglenone Forest (right)

Up on the Antrim plateau, Patrick and Miluic – though you get the feeling Miluic wouldn't have had much time for birdsong – would have heard the wheeping of the curlew. Common sandpipers and dippers dodged in the rushy glens in the company of willow-warblers and whitethroats much as they do today, but maybe the black-headed gulls and the dunlins which breed in the peat bog holes have come with man's scanty diggings. The peregrines have always been with us. Carpets of bluebells and primrose on upland slopes are often clues to vanished deciduous woodlands gone to intensive agriculture. Portglenone Forest between the Antrim plateau and the Bann is scattered with the old trees and alive with treecreeper and goldcrest.

The eel traps, Portna

The eel fisheries on the Bann, and in Lough Neagh, are the biggest in Europe and thus their ownership has been much in dispute over the centuries. Many of the traps (or skeaghs) here are in the same position, and are made of the same materials – hazel saplings – as those shown in seventeenth-century records. Three years after being spawned in the Sargasso sea the tiny elvers make their way up the Bann. Twelve years a-growing in Lough Neagh and they are ready for the Dutch table.

Saddler, Ballymena (opposite; top)

The great horse fairs of Ulster are gone. Their success sowed the seeds of their own destruction. So many horses were sold to the armies fighting the Napoleonic wars that the dealers had to import donkeys – not Irish at all it turns out – from Spain to replace them. But an affection for the horse rides in the folk memory.

The Crosskeys Inn (opposite; bottom)

You could do no better than call in on this early-nineteenth-century inn after a day's pike fishing on Lough Beg. Open turf fires, a maze of tiny rooms, low lintels, walls several feet thick and some of the best traditional music in the province. Fiddlers from the Glens exchanging musical phrases with taciturn lakesiders.

A basket of eels, Toome

A metre long and caught in the traps at Toome or Portna, or by longline on moonlit nights on the great flatness of Lough Neagh, eels are not a customary delight on the Ulster table. The delicatessen and the bistro will offer them smoked, but the smoking has probably taken place in Holland too.

Glenoe (above)

Glenoe lies right on the southern fringes of the Glynnes, or Glens, territory. The old road from Ballycarry, where Jemmy Orr, poet of the United Irishmen rebellion of 1798, came from, runs through it to Larne. Cotton-woolled in woods, splashed by four tiny waterfalls, it is proof, if you ever needed it, that there is more benefit to the eye in travelling the old roads. Motorways have their uses, for lorries and commercial travellers, pop-group roadies and commuters far from home. But Ulster's by-ways are for people.

Antrim Round Tower (left)

The Vikings drove tenth-century monks to build round towers such as this one across Ireland. The towers served as belfries and refuges for people and manuscripts; the manuscripts probably took precedence. The sixth-century monastery is gone but on Steeple Road the tower is a firm reminder of uncertain days.

Antrim and Sixmilewater (opposite)

Where the Sixmilewater runs into Lough Neagh, you can pick up a summer cruise on the Maid of Antrim. In the town's park you can marvel at the formality of the gardens laid out to plans by Le Notre, who designed the gardens at Versailles for Louis XIV. Lime and yew trees line the long water. Cyprus, chestnut, spruce and beech hang over the pool.

Ballygally, town and castle

Albert Clock (opposite)

BELFAST
and the Lagan Valley

Carrickfergus Castle

The history of Carrickfergus, and its castle, sitting on the northern shore of Belfast Lough, serves well to encapsulate a stylised history of the province and almost every town in it. We begin in untested myth. A king, Fergus McErc, is shipwrecked *c.*400 AD. In 1157 a Norman, de Courcy, builds a castle and is tricked out of it by a fellow Norman. The English crown intervenes. Famine at the end of the fifteenth century is followed by one hundred years of war. The English prepare 'the Plantation' in which they must put down the native O'Neills. A descendant of Sorley Boy MacDonnell's beheads Chichester, the castle's English strong man, and talks his way to a pardon.

In 1690 William of Orange, 'King Billy', lands to take the country in triumph from Catholic James. In 1760 the French, under Admiral Thurot, take the castle but don't like the food, and leave. In 1767 the port makes its second contribution to the Americas – Andrew Jackson's parents emigrate, his mother already pregnant. The first had been made in 1636 when, sixteen years after the *Mayflower,* the *Eaglewing* set sail with 140 pilgrims – but turned back. The third came in 1778 when John Paul Jones, father of the American Navy, captured the English brig *Drake* giving him America's first naval victory.

In 1797 William Orr, a worthy Presbyterian farmer, supported the United Irishmen like so many others of his religion and died for it. The nineteenth-century town grew with tradesmen and burghers, and with the Victorians came the shopkeepers and the railways and links to dormitory suburbs with pleasant views.

The twentieth century brought the widening of roads, the cutting off of the old seaport section from the rest of the town, developments seen everywhere, as old mercantile systems creak to a halt, new textile industries, based on synthetics, seek wider spaces, seaports turn to marinas and castles welcome foreign visitors rather than repel them.

Cave Hill, Belfast (also below)

Roll the dice for an image of Belfast:

*Red brick in the suburbs, white horse
on the wall,
Eyetalian marble in the City Hall
Oh stranger from England, why
stand so aghast?
May the Lord in His mercy be kind to Belfast.*

And again, Billy:

*My Aunt Jane she took me in,
She gave me tea out of her wee tin,
Half a bap, sugar on the top,
Three black lumps out of her wee shop.*

Roll it yourself:

*In a mean abode on the Shankill Road
Lived a man called William Bloat.
He had a wife, the curse of his life,
Who continually got his goat. . .*

He cut her throat with a razor, then
hung himself with a bed sheet. Only
she survived. . .

*For the razor blade was German made,
But the sheet was Irish linen.*

'Nuff said. There's Belfast. The
burghers of the thrusting Victorian
seaport immortalised in the ornate
solidity of the City Hall. The long red
brick streets for the workers, the folk
art of the dominant cult, the projected
cosiness of artisan communities
where village rule ran in a metropolis;
communities which knew a wastrel
when they saw him; the primacy of a
culture, fiercely British yet proud of
its other Irishness and its industrial
past.

Crown Liquor Saloon (opposite; top)

Grand Opera House (opposite; bottom)

Pavlova danced there. Those eminent Victorians, Beerbohm Tree and Forbes Robertson, trod its boards. Orson Welles did *Chimes at Midnight* and the divine Sarah, Sarah Bernhardt, graced the footlights. Yet when architect Robert McKinstry went into Belfast's Grand Opera House and Cirque in May 1975 it looked like a land-locked *Marie Celeste*. A chair floated in the flooded orchestra pit. The ashtrays screwed to the backs of the seats were still crushed full of old cigarette ends. Crates of unopened beer bottles sat behind the bar and, on the counter, four years of dust and spider webs topped the sour liquids in half-empty glasses. McKinstry had been chosen to blow the grime off Frank 'Matchless' Matcham's almost derelict creation. Matcham, Britain's and Ireland's most showmanlike and flamboyant theatrical architect, had lavished his gifts on this building and it had opened on December 3, 1895, with a performance of the pantomime *Bluebeard*, with all 2,500 seats taken.

Through two world wars and the intervening depression, the Opera House introduced generations to pantomime and Shakespeare, Donald Wolfit and Slim Whitman. But in the 1950s, malaise set in. Theatres across the country folded or turned to film. So the Grand Opera House became a cinema until it was finally put out of action altogether.

The story might have ended there. But, in 1973, the Ulster Architectural Heritage Society and the Arts Council of Northern Ireland called in McKinstry. In 1980, the theatre reopened, revealing Matcham's masterpiece once more to a delighted and nostalgic public. For its first Christmas back in business the Opera House brought back pantomime, the art form which had kept it open in the lean years between the wars. The pantomime was aptly chosen: *Cinderella*. Cinders from the ashes.

Just as they had always done, the stage door Johnnies took the chorus girls across the road to another of McKinstry's babies – the Crown Liquor Saloon – for an attempted snuggle in the snugs. The Crown, acquired by the National Trust, was also restored, under McKinstry.

Palm House, Botanic Gardens (above)

At the turn of the last century Belfast, like all other thriving Victorian ports, had its share of great commercial families whose sons turned to the sea for excitement and exploration.

There were botanist clergymen and the younger sons of landed gentry who learned obscure dialects and became customs officials and political advisers on the fringes of far distant empires. Sometimes they came back with an odd-shaped parcel. Sometimes the odd-shaped, odd-smelling parcel came back without them, later unwrapped to reveal glistening, strangely-shaped, exotic flora. But where to keep them? Where to find a micro-climate in which (even better) to propagate those which survived? The bulk of the surviving plants were xerophytes, which could withstand long periods of drought, or epiphytes which could take the water they need from the air around them. But still the majority perished from the salt spray if kept on deck, and from want of light and air if kept in the hold before they reached the Customs House (*right*). Then a certain Dr Ward hit on the idea of transporting plants in glass jars with a fair supply of wet soil and a seal to keep in the vapour. The good burghers of Belfast formed the first Wardian Society in the British Isles. The Royal Belfast Botanical Society, with fewer sources of new plants than the wealthier and more fashionable Dublin or London, must have been very pleased. Besides, the Society's Botanical Garden had something else very splendid going for it – its Palm House, now one of the oldest surviving curvilinear glasshouses in the British Isles. Its 22-metre-high wings represent the earliest known surviving work of the great iron founder Richard Turner whose skills can also be seen in the great Palm House at Kew Gardens in London, built in 1847, eight years after the foundation stone was laid in Belfast.

Customs House (above)

Tedford's Chandlery (right)

From that era of ship's chandlers, only Tedford's survives (*right*). But though the Palm House filled with plants and the layout of the gardens around it reflected the order which the nineteenth-century naturalists found in nature, all was not well with what was now called the Belfast Botanic and Horticultural Society. Frankly, they were short of money, and this led them to take desperate measures.

Sinclair Seamen's Presbyterian Church

Why, in 1840 it was even proposed that 'respectable tradesmen with their wives and families be admitted'. The resolution was not acted upon but, as the years went by, there were band concerts on Saturday afternoons and solid manufacturing companies bought tickets in bulk for the education and improvement of their workers. As early as 1838 there had been a fundraising fete and balloon ascent, and in 1842 an arranged 'submarine explosion' attracted 2,500 spectators. There were firework displays and troops of dancing Zulus and in 1891 a second balloonist, Captain Whelan, ascended with a lady parachutist, having first assured the crowd that she was both 'most respectable' and 'aged 25'. As one observer noted, a company which had set out to serve God had been forced to recognise mammon.

But somehow, over the years, the Palm House fell into neglect. The iron rusted, the great glass panes cracked, the doors were often closed. In 1971 the Ulster Architectural Heritage Society persuaded the authorities to rescue one of Ireland's most elegant buildings. One man, Charles Lanyon, must be remembered. He designed the Customs House, the Palm House, and Sinclair Seamen's Presbyterian Church (*above*).

Belfast from Craigantlet (below)

Indeed it was the behaviour of two men in the mid-nineteenth century which made Belfast what it is today; the providence of one and the improvidence of another. Lanyon's legacy to the city, and indeed to the province, is found in his constructions. Property speculator, engineer, opportunist, architect and politician he has given us not just the Palm House and Sinclair Seamen's but also the Queen's Bridge, Queen's University, the Northern Bank (Waring Street), the Trustee Savings Bank (Queen's Square), Assembly's College, Crumlin Road Gaol, Crumlin Road Courthouse and St Mark's Ballysillan, as well as the Glendun viaduct, much of the construction of the Antrim Coast Road and the

Frosses, those splendid avenues of fir trees holding the old bog road together between Ballymena and Ballymoney.

The other great moulder of Belfast was the second Marquess of Donegall. The improvident Marquess's debt grew so large that the city, literally, had to be sold, thus opening Lagan's banks to the banks and other speculators. Banks in those days came and went with alarming frequency and so men such as Lanyon were brought in to give them at least a solid appearance. They also gave us a straightforward street language. Never again would the citizens of Belfast have to wonder what a building was. Banks were solid, churches soared, prisons were impregnable, courthouses terrifying.

City Hall

A walk round Donegall Square can be an engaging experience. Just above you, on 10 Donegall Square South, you will find likenesses of Newton – the grave, Humbolt – the current, Jacquard – the weaver, Stevenson – the steam, Moore – the song, Watt – the other current, Michaelangelo – the magnificent, Columbus – the Americas, Washington – the cherry tree, Mercury – the ankles, Minerva – the wise, Shakespeare – the bard, Schiller – the poet and Homer – the legend. In the centre, dominating all, the ornate and imposing City Hall. Despite the city fathers having Queen Victoria pose, in statue as in stature, at the front, there can be no doubt that the best view of the building is from Linenhall Street at the rear.

Belfast, July 12 (right)

On the twelfth of July, in this city of pubs and churches, the Orangemen march. Like an army of old, on a long march, commemorating another army on another march. Derry, Aughrim, Enniskillen and the Boyne. White gloves, silk banners, hard hats, marching manners. The sabre, the fife and the drum. Commemorating the victory of Protestant King Billy, over Catholic King James in 1690, the march is held in 'glorious, pious and immortal memory' by many. But not by others.

'The Field', Edenderry (below)

The Lagan Canal (opposite)

Where Lagan stream sings
* lullaby*
There blooms a lily fair:
The twilight-gleam is in her eye,
The night is on her hair.
And, like a love-sick leanan-
  sidhe*,
She has my heart in thrall:
Nor life I owe, nor liberty,
For Love is lord of all.

Built in the 1760s with a levy raised on ale, the Lagan Canal, linked, in theory, Coleraine, Newry and the Shannon by inland waterway, to Belfast. The origins of this traditional air are lost but the penultimate line has echoes of the '98.

*leanan-sidhe/fairy-mistress

Hillsborough (left and opposite)

Founded by Arthur Hill, Hillsborough is preserved in the aspic of its mid-seventeenth-century origins. It rides on the delicate edge between the preciousness of becoming just another picturesque enclave of cosy antique shops, fashionable pubs and even more fashionable boutiques and remaining a living, working entity. Many of its residents are artists and writers, restaurateurs and entrepreneurs. The windows of the houses which have not yet become boutiques present carefully planned arrangements of geraniums and brass, busy lizzies and frilly ferns.

See the Gothic Hillsborough Fort dating from 1650, then the Palladian Tholsel or market house, now housing the Petty Sessions, and beyond it, the sprawling, rambling ashlar buildings of Government House and the Shambles, once a cattle mart, now a cloister for summer art exhibitions.

Back down the slope, up a long limetree avenue, is the most beautiful Gothic church in Ireland, graced with two splendid organs, one a Snetzler dating from 1772. And you still haven't strolled round the forest park to watch the mallard dip and the trout rise in the shadow of the tall trees. Maybe you should come back again. My ancestors evidently did.

The Lagan in winter

At the Ulster Folk Museum (opposite)

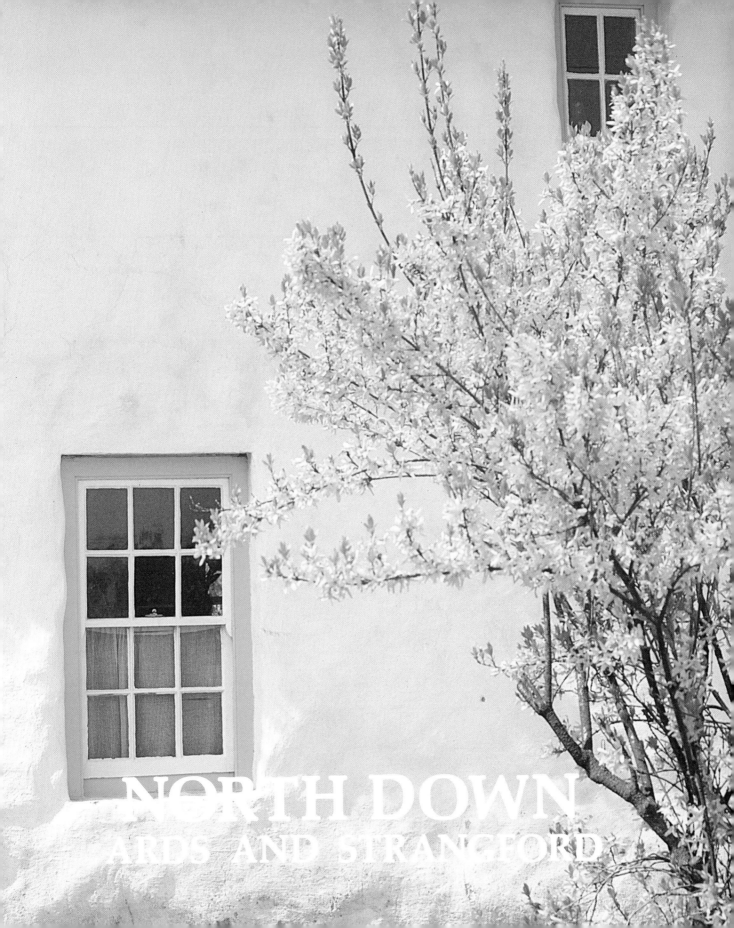

NORTH DOWN
ARDS AND STRANGFORD

Folk and Transport Museum, The Rectory (opposite)

For a really reliable shibboleth ask an Ulster acquaintance to pronounce the letter 'h'. Catholics will probably say 'haitch', Protestants 'aitch'. It's the result of separate schooling, Catholic schools leaning to the Irish pronunciation, Protestants to the conventional British. Your acquaintance may well inform you that he 'digs with the other foot'. 'How interesting,' you murmur back, wondering why he wants to discuss gardening when you thought you were going to sort out the Irish question once and for all. Should you ever find yourself in such a predicament, see the Ulster Folk and Transport Museum. Once there, go straight to the sturdy, nineteenth-century water-powered Coalisland spade mill and all will be revealed. A hundred years ago a spade mill such as this would have produced well over a hundred types of spade, each one suited, by ergonomic evolution, to the particular character of a locality's soil or peat.

The Spade Mill (left)

A spade could be right-footed or left-footed and rural communities of the day were isolated and tended to be one religion or the other. Thus a man from another district, of another faith, became a man 'who digs with the other foot' and the expression is as much as part of today's language as ever it was.

But, of course, the Folk Museum is much more than that. Over the 136 acres, the vernacular of Ulster's past has been re-created, stone by stone, ranging from the one-room earthen-floored, thatch-roofed, one-windowed Meenagarragh Cottier's House from the Sperrin Mountains, through the

continued
Cruckaclady Farmhouse with a byre for the cattle tucked under the bedroom (like the garage in a modern house), to the prosperous one-time rectory from near Toome Bridge. Each house has been re-created on a site not unlike its original setting and furnished with artefacts of its period. Most days a turf fire burns in each grate and the guide can tell you everything you could want to know about the houses and the life-style of their former occupants.

Crawfordsburn Country Park (opposite)

**Helen's Tower
(above and right)**

*Helen's Tower here I stand
Dominant over sea and land
Son's love built me, and I hold
Mother's love in lettered gold.*

Tennyson's lines, with others by Carlyle, Browning, Kipling and Wilfrid Scawen Blunt hang in Helen's Tower in the Clandeboye estate, threnodies to Helen Selina Sheridan, grand-daughter of Richard Brinsley and mother of the first Marquess of Dufferin and Ava. A replica tower, with another poem – the word 'Ulster's' replacing the word 'Mother's' – remembers, at Thiepval, the desperate losses of the 36th (Ulster) Division at the Somme.

44

Bangor by the sea

Ah, Bangor. Ice cream 'sliders' and stucco villas, bay windows, chips, a row round the bay in varnished clinker-built rowing boats. Small boys fishing off the pier in the summer sun. Girls out 'in their figures'. We've never had a Betjeman to do you justice, Bangor, just our own McGonagall, Julius Leckey McCullough Craig, who wrote:

. . . away from the city's dust and clangour,
Take the boat train down to Bangor.

Yacht shrouds rattling, trippers handbags. Ah, Bangor.

Bangor shop

Baps, wheaten farls, soda farls. Barmbracks, 'tatie bread, currant bread.

But the soda bread is your only man. Toasted, buttered hot, till it drips. Buttered cold and smothered with rhubarb jam. Fried on Saturday morning in dripping. Topped with an egg. Mug of tea. Happiness. Walk the dog. Pick stuck grass clippings off the golf shoes. Might have a pint later. Watch the lads play rugby. Have another pint. Go home. D'ye fancy a big fry?

See me? See Bangor!

Farm at Orlock

. . . as in shipping forecast. . . Malin. . . Prestwick. . . Corsewall Point. . . Larne. . . Orlock, South, 5, Visibility good, 16 miles. One thousand and eleven, falling slowly. . . Killough. . . no report from Kilkeel. . . Ronaldsway. It's eleven ten at night. On Radio Ulster medium wave, on 1341 kilohertz. The inshore waters shipping forecast as at 9.00 pm this evening, all that most of us ever hear about Orlock Point or any of the little coastguard stations, some Victorian and imperial, some more functional and less memorable, around the rocky coast. Inland, tight solid huddles of white-washed farm buildings crouch where farm buildings have crouched for centuries between the drumlins of east Down.

The roads and lanes are narrow, the hedges high, the soil rich. Greylag geese, tempted sometimes from the rich feeding on the sloblands of Strangford Lough, graze on the glinting grass. The roads wind, untouched in width for centuries. Both long-established farmers and newcome yachts-people guard their privacy. Sometimes, on the twisting roads, suddenly the car wheels are slicked with a flurry of mud and straw as you traverse a clachan where the farm outbuildings spread both sides of the narrow way. In late summer you beware of great hay wagons lumbering sunset-wards. Frantic dogs snap ritually at your radials, cows scratch their necks on the barbed wire; but the sea is over the next rise.

Donaghadee Harbour

Ballycopeland Windmill

Sir John Rennie is better known for his designs for the Eddystone Lighthouse than for his work on the splendid solid edifice at Donaghadee, where the deep harbour welcomed Peter the Great, Czar of all the Russias, John Keats, Daniel Defoe, spying for the Crown, and hundreds of thousands of other travellers, when it was still the main packet port from Scotland. At that time the hundreds of windmills which dotted the grain-rich lands of the Ards Peninsula must have been navigation marks almost as useful as lighthouses for sailors east and west of the peninsula.

The coast, Ballywalter (below)

Mustard-coloured lichens roughen the black rocks, butterfish wriggle, stirring up silt to hide in after the lifted stone lets bladderwrack fall. The shallow beaches between the tiny harbours of Ballywalter and Ballyhalbert are places for summer football – a grey pullover, a blue anorak the goal posts. Windsurfers wrestle with flapping mainsails. A stubbed toe brings granny, feet splatting on the wet sand, to fractious groups of unsuccessful sand-castle builders. Kettles boil on Calor stoves, tomatoes soak the white bread sandwiches.

View from the Temple of the Winds, Mountstewart

Every large Irish lough should have 365 islands, one for every day of the year. It is a felicitous and easily remembered arrangement and so it seems uncommonly ungenerous, in the face of such exact local knowledge, for Admiralty Chart 2156 to credit Strangford Lough, a twenty-nine-kilometre by six-kilometre inlet, with only seventy islands. The rich lands of Down attracted not just the smallholder and the tenant farmer, part fisherman, part crofter, but also those who found ways of finding favour with the Crown. The area is dotted with the extravagances of the privileged of the eighteenth and nineteenth centuries. The first Marquess of Londonderry bought his son, Lord Castlereagh, the man who sent Wellington off to sort out the Peninsular Wars, a seat in the Commons for £30,000 in 1790; £30,000 in 1790! He also built the Temple of the Winds, an almost exact replica of the original in Athens, as a summer dining room, with stone from Scrabo hill across this water.

Under Scrabo

Castlereagh was labelled 'Bloody' for his involvement in putting down the '98 rebellion. He is also often put forward as a man of peace for establishing the Treaty of Vienna, perhaps a tenuous forerunner of the United Nations – but he also fought a pistol duel with Canning and ended his own life by cutting his throat, not with a razor blade like William Bloat, but with a pen-knife. Later, in the spirit of an age where wealth bent nature as it suited it, the family had Charles Lanyon build a tower on Scrabo in memory of the 3rd Marquess who commanded a brigade of hussars under Sir John Moore.

The view from Scrabo (opposite)

Mountstewart (above)

The reins of power were few in those days. The 3rd Marquess's second wife was daughter of a Countess of Antrim, a MacDonnell. Her daughter married a Marlborough and thus, somewhere, in the genetic codes for power and dominance those of Sorley Boy, seed of Vikings, mingle with Winston in his War Room.

Mountstewart was the Londonderry home, and is now in the care of the National Trust. The 7th Marquess's wife had the sculptures on Dodo Terrace cut as anthropomorphic symbols for her friends. Winston was the warlock.

Mermaid on Dodo Terrace (right)

When the sun dipped behind the Mournes and a shadow chilled the Promenade the pierrots came out to play, in Newcastle by the sea. The donkeys had been turned by the same sea wet wind which drove their tiny customers away and which etched patiently into the cast iron of the bandstand.

'Oh, Oh, Oh, what a lovely war!'

'I say, I say, my dog's got no nose.'

'How does he smell?'

'Absolutely terrible!'

The pierrots' ghosts laid, the bandstand has been moved to Rowallane Gardens to the spot where Rowallane's founder, the Rev John Moore, preached.

Rowallane Gardens (right)

Window, Greyabbey (right)

Rowallane suffers from plagues of old ladies, sweeping the bushes like hosts of locusts, sharp elegant scissors rolled tight in their lavender-water-scented lace handkerchiefs: they prey on the rare shrubs, a slip here, a cutting there, to be folded away into the rich loam soil of their south Belfast gardens. But *Magnolia watsonii, M. dawsoniana, M. mollicomata, Hydrangea sargentiana* and *Philesia buxifolia* blossom between the prize rhododendrons.

But there are wild rhododendrons enough for most of us, and fuschia escaped, and veronica in the calm bee-loud hedges of the Ards. For there is something in the salt air, and summer sun and sandy soil of the Down coast which favours these shrubs particularly. Sometimes their origins are easily enough traced; a ruined cottage, a broken garden wall, the rusty gate, the grassed-over beech avenue to an old roofless house half-hidden in a hilltop coppice by a 'fairy fort'.

Greyabbey house (below)

The Harbour, Killyleagh

A harbour is amongst the most potent of icons. The seeds of blood, love, sweat, tears, birth and death, greeting, parting all hang in the still air or are tossed in the whipped seas. Above this harbour, a stile in Killowen old graveyard touched Helen Selina Sheridan – who herself, in turn, inspired Helen's Tower – to write, at the time of famine and emigration:

> I'm very lonely now, Mary,
>   For the poor make no new friends,
> But, O, they love the better still,
>   The few our father sends,
> And you were all I had, Mary,
>   My blessing and my pride.
> There's nothing left to care for now,
>   Since my poor Mary died.

There must be something special too in the air round Killyleagh which is good for breeding more than fuschia and veronica. Edward Hincks, who decoded the Rosetta Stone, lived in the rectory here. Hans Sloane, whose collection was the kernel of the British Museum, was born here too. Above the town Charles Lanyon gave the Hamilton family a Rhine schloss where John de Courcy, whose wife built Greyabbey, first made fortifications.

Public house, Killyleagh

Coal boats still moor at Killyleagh pier and there is small trade in dredging for scallops, potting for Dublin Bay prawns and taking sport fishermen to deep holes in the lough bottom for large skate, and so pubs often have a piece of fishing net, or a green globe glass float or a man who can clean a spark-plug on an outboard.

55

Public house, Portaferry

Strangford Lough

You could potter the summer away in quiet bays between these islets, steep-sloped to the north, shallow to the south, just as the glaciers left them; for company, a rabbit, a tern, a mast, a sail somewhere in the heat-hazed distance. Sit back, listen to the distant tractor over the next hill.

If the terns dive for fry, feather for mackerel. If they don't, don't. Then come back in the winter and marvel at the 4,000 brent geese 'summering' here before their return to the Arctic. Wintering dunlins top the 20,000 mark and if someone totted up the oyster-catchers, knot, curlews and other waders they would find over 100,000. Pintails, mergansers, teal, golden eye, mallard and widgeon complete the winter's wealth. Take pub intervals between species.

Castleward (opposite)

Gulls, Portavogie Harbour

There is more to a
fisherman's harbour than
is seen through the
steamed-up window of the
Sunday car, more even
than the half-rolled-down
window, the tossed butt,
the crumpled tabloid and
the oh-did-you-ever-see-
that-woman's-hat? More
than the choc off the choc
ice now flaked between
you and the seat, more
than the apple core too big
for the ashtray, too small
for the wading through the
sea's puddles to the distant
trash-can.

Portavogie Harbour

Read the loneliness in a
fishing boat's name,
measure in your mind's
eye the thickness of a
hemp hawser. Look over
the breakwater and watch
the broad prows plough
towards you. In the boxes
by the fish auction, name
each species. Cod and
haddock, easy enough.
Plaice, sole, dab and
flounder? Bright red spots
on the plaice, dull orange
on the flounder; lemon
soles have smooth skins,
Dover soles one elliptical
spot behind the head.
Dabs are small and
freckled. OK?

Downpatrick, streets meeting (opposite)

Downpatrick is the Ulster
town, so simmered down,
so compressed, to the
essential ingredients of all
Ulster towns that many
Ulster people scarcely
notice it at all. By contrast,
what a delight it can be to
the stranger. The Georgian
doorways, the ornately-
tiled butcher's shop, the
solid proportions of the
small commercial hotel.
The street names holding
all of the north's
history. . . Irish Street,
English Street, Scotch
Street, Market Street. The
Judge's Lodgings, the
Downe Hunt Club, the
Southwell Charity
Almshouse and School,
the Assembly Rooms, the
Cathedral with the graves
of both St Patrick and
Thomas Russell, a leader
of the '98.

A racecourse, odd
Victorian pubs and
legendary curing wells
complete the package,
most of it nestling in
hollows between two close
hills. The walk from the
butcher's, up English
Street to the Cathedral and
back is one of the most
satisfying urban walks in
the north. To pick an equal
you would have to walk
the length of Portaferry,
looking across the narrows
to Strangford – or vice
versa. Better try all three.

Cottage at Kearney

Slieve Loughshannagh (opposite)

MOURNE
COUNTRY

The Mournes

Foley's Bridge, Tollymore (opposite)

Light changes constantly in the Mournes as clouds bowl their shadows over the rough hillsides and the solid white farmhouses in rushy valleys. Pass in the morning and the fresh white-wash is almost too bright to look at; a minute later everything can be in a cold shadow. Hours later it certainly will be. Further up, above the cornfield line, above the sheep-cropped grass you can sit in perfect solitude on a dry-stone wall warmed in the sun. A slight wind sings through the stone tracery, a grasshopper cheeps, a lark spirals, a hawk hunts. Listen harder, for a stream trickles.

The Mournes are mostly gentle, a family of sleepy giants out for an evening stroll, and from the top of a peak you may look north to the sweep of Dundrum Bay with its de Courcy castle; out to sea, east to the Isle of Man, south to Howth Head, north-west to Lough Neagh. Was it here that Finn McCool of the Causeway stood, having scooped out a great clod of earth – leaving Lough Neagh – and skimmed it across the waters to form the Isle of Man? Down below, in Newcastle, with its promenade and beach donkeys, is where Percy French stood, enabling him to note, in metre and clef, that this is 'Where the Mountains of Mourne sweep down to the sea'.

Tollymore Forest Park is full of delights in what was once the most satisfactory demesne in Ireland. The succession of little rubble-built bridges, Clonachullion, Horn, Parnell's, Maria's, Altavady, Hore's, Ivy and Foley's; the apparently natural rock cascades on the Spinkwee River, the Georgian barns, the Barbican Gate, Lord Limerick's folly gateposts, the subtleties of view, ride and walk. Near Foley's bridge an inscription runs:

Here, in full light, the russet plains extend,
There, wrapped in clouds, the bluish hills ascend,
Even the wild heath displays her purple dyes,
And, 'midst the desert, fruitful fields arise.

Castlewellan Forest Park is much more formal. No sprightly little bridges here. Whilst in Tollymore Nature was gently and subtly rearranged, here, between Slieve Croob and the Mournes proper, arrangements are much more strict. The town of Castlewellan is strict too, with upper and lower market squares, but the regimented wide streets and squares are softened by well-spaced old chestnut trees.

The countryside about is dotted with lakes and the ring fort at Drumena, almost on the shores of Lough Island Reavy, is well-defined and worth a brisk walk round after a pot of tea, or a pint. Walks inside the Forest Park are plentiful. There will be those who will be content with the symmetry of the Grange, courtyard and parking lot, and for others the Arboretum will be heaven.

Arboretum, Castlewellan Forest Park

In the autumn, when there are still trout fishermen out on the lake and schoolkids walk giggling in male and female groups, you can – with due caution – pick a basketful of common puffballs, ceps, shaggy ink-caps and chanterelles under the old deciduous trees, the oaks and the beech, out on the lawns or on the lakeside banks. Take them home, fry them gently with tiny chips of bacon. Serve on diamonds of brown bread fried in the juices. A squirt of lemon and you've the second part of morning's heaven. But, before your basket is full, study the ducks and drakes on the lake, count red and grey squirrels, watch the pony-trekkers, ponder on what goes on behind the walls of the Scottish-baronial castle and even hike up to the top of tiny Slievenaslat to make the muscles tired enough to feel they've done something.

Castlewellan Lake (left) and Castle (opposite)

Towards Hare's Gap

Deer's Meadow, Hare's Gap, Brandy Pad, Cock Mountain, Butter Mountain, Rowan Tree River, Pigeon Rock River, Crocknafeola, Slievemageoh. Translations, mis-translations; mis-remembered ends of old people's stories, rural idiocies, rural charms. The Mournes, like other wilder parts of this island, came partly under the cartographer's eye and re-emerged, part anglicised, part not. Brian Friel, the north's most famous playwright, wrote movingly of such matters in *Translations*.

Just drive slowly here on the narrow roads. Respect the foolish jumping sheep and the taciturn shepherd. Admire the solid round gateposts, the tops conical, people might tell you, to make sure the evil fairies slip off before they can settle down to a serious spell of crop-cursing and lamb-wasting. Pick a spot where you can line up a long stone wall against the skyline in the setting sun. Note the weave and weft, inspiration for some tweedy sweater. And if you walk, seek out good maps, stout boots and good advice. Trace part of the Ulster Way if you like, but let someone know where you are going and when you hope to be back. There is a Mournes Rescue Service but let them lie a-bed.

Royal County Down, Newcastle

Sport is more than the statistics of points scored and yards covered, and ratings of the best are best left to moustachioed men in club-houses to argue over between gins and tonics. However this Royal links, one of three in Northern Ireland, was rated number one on a list of one to fifty of the best in the world outside America by an authoritative group of sports writers.

Hilltown

Not just any hill town, but Hilltown, taking its name from the Hill family of Hillsborough and not, as you would reasonably suppose, from the lovely dark Mournes in whose foothills it lies. Flat caps, collie dogs, good stout, hard-bargaining and a bit of 'crack' are the order of the day at the autumn sheep fair. Spare, raw people, sinewy from a lifetime of hill-walking; clear-eyed from watching far-off ewes. Strong-jawed and sparse, courteous and welcoming with the dignity of mountainy men, closer to God than valley city folks. Early autumn is a good time for the Mournes, for, apart from the sheep fair, and the ceps under the oak trees, herring-boats will be docking at Annalong and Kilkeel.

Kilkeel Harbour

Kilkeel Harbour (opposite)

The River Bann

Some say Comber spuds are the best, some opt for Kilkeel's, boiled till the jackets split and they laugh at you. These are great balls of flour not like the little yellow, hard and soapy chaps favoured in Belgium and Holland. A little salt, a knob of butter and what more could you want but a plate of Kilkeel herrings fried till dark and crispy brown in a dry pan?

There remains the question then of what way to treat the prawns, so plentiful from these little east coast ports, now that the prawn cocktail is so rightly held in some derision.

These are not the 'Dublin Bay' prawn of Portaferry, not the *langoustine* (Fr.) *cigala* (Sp.) *langostim* (Pr.) *kaisergranat* (Gr.) or *noorse kreeft* (Du.) but rather the humbler *crevette rose, gamba, camarao branco, sagegarnele, orsteurgarnaal*. Boil, peel, then fry in butter whilst opening a jar of cumin in the same room. Add a smidgin of Bushmills whiskey just before serving, hot.

The Bann rises in the Mournes, up near Lough Shannagh with its fine white sandy beach, and makes its way past Rathfriland, Banbridge, Gilford and Portadown to Lough Neagh at Bannfoot. There are good fish in it, trout, some big pike and, down nearer the Lough, shoals of roach. On its way it would have driven engines for the linen mills when the country, from here to Belfast, was linen, linen all the way. Rathfriland is a hilltop 'Plantation' town and Patrick Brontë, father of all the Brontës, preached not far away.

Some castles have a greedy hard majesty, some just have brawn and sit there saying brutal unsubtle words to the peasantry, some have style and nerve. Obviously picturesque, and equally obviously of strategic value, Narrow Water Castle cost the English garrison £361.4s.2d. to erect in 1560. The Magennises, local lads who were always flexing their muscles, held it for a while. Pretty but functional, with a murder hole and other practical devices.

Narrow Water Castle

Harvest near Rostrevor

Ulster people are fond of naming Ulster families who put their boy into the White House. The north claims Andrew Jackson, James Knox Polk, James Buchanan, Andrew Johnson, Ulysses Simpson Grant, Chester Alan Arthur, Grover Cleveland, Benjamin Harrison, William McKinley, Theodore Roosevelt and Woodrow Wilson. Carter and Nixon were both making enquiries before they departed. But another Ulsterman made it to the White House in an even more dramatic way. He was Major-General Robert Ross from Rostrevor. In 1814, fighting for the British, he won at Bladensburg, burned the Capitol and ate the dinner President Maddison had hastily abandoned in the White House.

Bar the sombre intrusion of the Mournes, the County of Down is a county of gentle hills, drumlins; like eggs set in salt. And across the land ring-forts and Neolithic tombs dot the skylines. The walls of early Christian churches sit in fields of cows. Unexplained stone circles interrupt the hussocky grasses and pillars put up by pagans were carved, later, to Christian rules OK. Monks built round towers, and Vikings, coming up Carlingford Lough, and time, knocked them down.

Carlingford Lough from Flagstaff Hill (opposite)

Kingfisher

The Mall, Armagh (opposite)

The County of
ARMAGH

Across Ulster's flowery vale the two cathedrals, icons of the two cultures, observe each other quietly – twin hubs to Ireland's ellipse. And much revolves round here. Cuchullain, our greatest hero, took on the Connaught army man by man, cutting down each one before meeting his own death.

Ptolemy wrote of Navan Fort outside the city. Brian Boru lies in the churchyard at the Protestant Cathedral, killed at the Battle of Clontarf, shattering the Vikings. At Yellow Ford on the Callan River Hugh O'Neill beat the English for the last time. The Catholic St Patrick's is Gothic, the Protestant St Patrick's partly medieval, near the foundations of Patrick's own church. Grimacing gargoyles glower above, the nave slants rakishly askew and, in the Chapter House and crypt, St Patrick, in statue, looks seriously at the visitor. A topless Queen Macha and other heroes of an antic age lean and twist in the shadows. In the Cathedral library, Jonathan Swift's annotations to a copy of *Gulliver's Travels* fascinate the bookish. A sense of time and age pervades, for Queen Macha had a fort nearby in 600 BC.

The little County Museum, in the Mall, has an air of brown and brassbound quiet but the Book of Armagh, ninth-century life of St Patrick, is in Trinity College Dublin. An Armagh librarian pawned it in 1608 for £5.

Armagh, from St Patrick's Catholic Cathedral

Armagh's Georgian Mall is Ulster's most exquisite 'square' and there is nothing finer than to laze on the summer lawns, sipping cider from Armagh's apples, listening to the 'thuk' of leather on willow. The shape of the Mall itself is, fittingly, like a bat's blade in profile. The progress along it from the elegant Court House, built at the birth of the nineteenth century, to the imposing gaol at the other end may not always have been so relaxing. Sights of such processions may have been improving, though, for the lads of the Royal School whose classrooms date from 1774 or for the pupils of Drelincourt's School, 1740, or indeed for the apprentices at the Observatory, 1791. Much of the elegance of the houses in this part of the city is due to a local architect, Francis Johnston, and the doorways are as elegant and the glazing bars on the windows as fine as those in Dublin.

The Mall, Armagh City (right and below)

Some would choose the apple's blossom, some the red-green shine of the fruit itself as chief pleasures of this orchard county. But sit by a face-hot turf fire on a winter evening, and shine your nose with a Bramley's wax, and crunch into its ice-cold, juice-sharp flesh and you have a greater pleasure.

Bramley 'cookers' (left)
Bramley blossom (below)

Bessbrook viaduct

White smoke over green fields.
The 'S' class 4-4-0, number 171
Slieve Gullion is the pride of the
Railway Preservation Society of
Ireland's collection of steam
locomotives. The railway viaduct
at Bessbrook is the longest in
Ireland. From the top of Slieve
Gullion mountain itself, just down
the line, you can almost see the
smoke of the engine all the way
from Belfast to Dublin.
On another part of their excursion
steam afficionados would no doubt
have shaken heads at match
anglers pulling hundreds of
pounds weight of tiny roach from
the river Bann, just beside the
railway bridge. What a very odd
way to pass the day, you can hear
them say above the clickety-
clack-Dublin-and-back of the
iron wheels.

Match fishing on the Bann

The art of the stuccodore

What a splendid name for a
splendid profession. Michael
Stapleton, stuccodore, made his
name with elegant circles and
segments, husk chains and
reeding, floating classical figures,
on the plaster walls of St Stephen's
Green in Dublin at the same time as
Francis Johnston and the Ensor
brothers were designing that city's
other squares and some of the
houses of Armagh. When the
National Trust were restoring the
drawing room at Ardress House
they were able to trace the
stuccodore's original drawings and
thus bring the room back to its
original colours.
The subjects of the other plaques
around the walls – Winter,
Autumn, Spring and Summer – are
stock ones, and so may also be seen
on the Dublin house walls.

Ardress, Derrymore, the Argory,
the 'modest' houses of the business
classes of the eighteenth and
nineteenth centuries, are little
lacunae of peace and calm, leisure
and privilege. Park in the
otherwise empty car parks, see
children in yellow wellies on the
gravel drives, wide polished
floorboards, and families from the
nearby villages checking out folk
scandals of the landed families
with the houndstooth-jacketed
National Trust administrators.
George Ensor married into the
family which owned Ardress and
re-modelled the original 1660
building in 1770. The central facade
dates from 1660, as does the main
portion of the house looked at from
the calm gardens.

Ardress House (right)
Slieve Gullion (opposite)

Fisherman's paradise

Lough Erne (opposite)

LAKELAND

A plaque on the wall of Portora Royal School commemorates Henry Francis Lyte, composer of 'Abide with me' – 'King George V's favourite hymn'. Other old boys include Oscar Wilde and Samuel Beckett. Dominating the other end of this hilly island town towers a monument to General Galbraith Lowry-Cole, hero of the Peninsular Wars. Maguire's Castle and the Watergate commemorate the Maguires who were notable for a particularly Irish combination of taking no prisoners and having great parties. Nothing remains to commemorate Ceithleann, wife of Balor of the Mighty Blows, no mean warrior herself, who put down the De Dannan 2,000 years before the birth of Christ, but in Ceithleann, the warlord Maguires, the Coles their Plantation successors, plus British regiments and the minor public school you have something of the history of this island town.

Enniskillen, the main street (left and below)

82

The Watergate (opposite)

Castlecoole (opposite)

Fermanagh lakeland is a land of gentle, still and flowing waters, a land of placid lakes and wooded islands. Big lakes and little lakes, broad loughs and narrow loughs. And between them, past the white-washed cottages run the rivers, between banks where the dun brown, head down, fly be-ribboned cattle, move hock-high in reedy shallows to the gentle slopes. Reeds and reed mace, bulrushes and flag iris clothe other banks and the willow and the alder, the ash and the sycamore dip shadows on the water meadow. . .
corncrakes crake, warblers warble. . . and the waters themselves are an empire of fat fish waiting to be caught, waiting there, swimming there, breeding there, deep down at the edge of green fields, through the farmer's lane, past his haystacks. . .
So fish there on a spring evening, with the only sound the panting of a passing collie, the ticking of the freewheel on the farmer's pushed bicycle. . . the wind in his willows. Or the gentle voices across the fish-thick water, mingling with the softest sound of passing cruisers.
Many a fisherman has kept his family happy visiting Castlecoole or telling them they're really here for a cruising holiday, and. . . so. . . he might as well bring his rods along too. Many a mallard competes for the fishing but their tiny share leaves a lot left over for you. Anyway there are plenty of fish to go round, for the Ulsterman, if you leave out pike, thinks of coarse fish angling as something he did as a boy. . . once. . . long ago.
And a close season for coarse is something we never got around to investigating in Northern Ireland. You can fish to your heart's content through the four seasons. For a few pounds you can collect all the rod licences and permits you'll need for a whole year's coarse angling and

then our lakes are your lakes to share with the few of us out in boats after pike maybe. Or with summer's seasonal holidaymakers, but the lakes and the rivers are so many, and so wide, that you'll rarely get close enough to see the whites of their eyes, just the whites of their sails.
On Melvin cold hands clutch at salmon rods in the February sleet, or hunt the elusive gillaroo at summer dusk. Trout rise in little tributaries and across the tiny rounded loughs the celandine glows beside the wild mint and the marsh orchid, and Frankie McPhillips, of Tempo, ties the best of trout and salmon flies.

Any winter evening, any lake shore, Lough Macnean perhaps, you can fish for pike almost anywhere. You dead-bait with mackerel or herring, or small roach, or use a small perch live-baited, just hooked through the upper lip. And you'll end up with one snapping round your ankles in the wet bottom of a tiny dinghy on some tiny reed-fringed lough, the cold rain and the brusque wind on your face.

Then you can come back in the summer to a willow-dipped, alder-shadowed, lily-dappled pond, and as the shadows creep forward and the pond stills, bar a moorhen's 'wake', as the evening breeze folds, another jack pike's down to another dead-bait, making you remember other fish. And what does the fish remember? Hours in the warm shallows waiting for a passing meal, a fish, a frog, your friend the waterhen?

Put him in again and don't make it his last supper.

Tempo village (left)   85

Carved figures, White Island

The islands and shores of Lough Erne are dotted with ruined churches, old graveyards. The people here were head-hunters once and the severed head on a spear, or formed from stone, meant power and terror. Many of the carvings now have a Christian provenance but the old gods left art and mystery across this great lake. Till the last century carved heads were still being chiseled from the local stones and strange faces look down from old walls. Sometimes the faces are the older.

Church, White Island

The figures, now set in the wall, were carved in pairs, under the direction of one master, as supports for pulpits and an altar. From right: an unfinished figure; Christ the warrior; Christ with griffins; King David, singing psalms; St Anthony; Christ with gospels; Sheila-na-gig, a smiling and shameless temptress. Not surprisingly this last figure has given archaeologists, Christian and otherwise, problems.

Janus figure, Boa Island

Earlier than the White Island figures, the single-headed, double-headed, even treble-headed stone figures of this vast waterland are troublesome icons both for the academics and for those who sit in silence, alone with them in summer sun, or winter chill. The two stone faces, the Belsen arms and legs, the single phallus, have a heavy power. Seamus Heaney wrote:

> *January god*
> *. . .Who broke the water, the hymen*
> *With his great antlers –*
> *There reigned upon each ghost tine*
> *His familiars,*
>
> *The mothering earth, the stones*
> *Taken by each wave,*
> *The fleshy aftergrass, the bones*
> *Subsoil in each grave.*

Round Tower, Devenish Island (opposite)

Up on Benaughlin, the mountain of the horse, you can just see the faint outline of a white horse in the limestone. In Marble Arch glen, primrose and bluebell grow beneath the rowan and the elder. But underground the mysteries commence. Waters bubble and red- and yellow-hard-hatted cavers emerge from behind the guelder rose, like brash handkerchiefs from the magician's hat where the Claddah river ran, in caverns measureless to man. Clinks and grikes abound and swallow-holes dot the plateaus. On summer Sundays the go-to-meeting suits of farmers merge with the anoraks of backpackers and the Gucci handbags of barristers' wives. Guided tours take in the stalactites and stalagmites.

Lough Macnean (opposite)
Marble Arch Caves (below)

The Fiddler's Stone

'Hang the harpers, wherever found,' commanded Elizabeth I, a blind harper being a prerequisite of every great Irish family. But the Flight of the Earls left the harpers without protectors and though Cromwell was a little less peremptory – wandering musicians were tolerated as long as their papers were in order – the loss of patronage, the death of polyphonic music after Palestrina and the adoption of major and minor keys on the continent left the Irish music to the mists of time. However, Edward Bunting had transcribed the harpers' airs in Lanyon's Assembly Rooms at the Belfast Harp Festival of 1792 in impossible keys (for harpists), so the music survived through to this century.

It even survived the folk revival of the late sixties, a mixture of flower-power, sandals and fat bearded men jumping up and down, Aran-besweatered, shiny-beer-faced, shouting 'Fine girrel ye arre'. Dennis McCabe, though, did not survive. Fiddler to the Count of Milan, he fell drunk and fiddling into the lake and drowned. This stone is his memorial.

The music's rhythms could be a jig in 6/8 time, or from a man singing, *sean-nos,* in the old style, as he cut turf in the bog or walked the mountains at Navar.

Bringing in the turf
Lough Navar Forest Park (opposite)

The Erne

The Sperrins (opposite)

The
SPERRINS

Smithy, Ulster-American Folk Park (right)

The skeins of an Ulster-American heritage trail wind along the green river valleys of Ulster. There were two great waves of emigration; in the nineteenth century Catholic, in the eighteenth Protestant. The Ulster-American Folk Park, at Camphill, outside Omagh, on the fringe of the Sperrins, is a memorial to that eighteenth-century depopulation, when Presbyterian settlers, who had come from Scotland a century before, found themselves thwarted by the English establishment. The Park recreates the land they left, the wilderness they conquered.

Wellbrook Beetling Mill

Dissenting, and exporting natural talent, have long been Ulster traits. Linen-making was another. The valleys of little rivers are dotted with the great stones of long-silent mills where girls and children worked impossible hours to provide stiff lengths of white and shiny damask tablecloths to catch the claret stains at the tables of the great. In beetling, huge wooden mallets, on axles driven by water, beat the cloth to its rich sheen. The National Trust has restored and operates the Mill, the Ballinderry river bubbles and gurgles at the wheel, trout idle in the pools.

Meeting House, Ulster-American Folk Park (opposite)

Strabane pub

A priest is a short, weighted stick for delivering the last rites to a brown trout. A curate, by contrast, is the man who pours a good pint for you, and puts up a half 'un on the high, solid wood counter of a good house. Mirrors advertising long-lost whiskeys back the barman, and freely available is irrelevant and inaccurate advice on fishing methods, the way to the nearest 'giant's grave' and the state of tomorrow's weather as judged from the gait of a cow by the gate.

Caledon, on the Blackwater

The O'Neills, whose power-base was on the Blackwater, and who resisted both Christianity and the English, had their last great champion in Hugh who was 'of a meane stature, but a strong body, able to indure labours, watching and hard fare, being withal industrious and active, valiant, affable, and apt to manage great affaires, and of high, dissembling, subtile, and profound wit, and so many deemed him borne either for the good or ill of his countery'. You could find a man like that in a Tyrone pub, any day.

Omagh (opposite)

The O'Neills weren't quite finished, after Hugh, but it wasn't long before the 'Plantation' was complete and Captain Ormond Leigh had built a place of good import where a confluence of rivers forms the Strule. Across Tyrone, and in the county of Londonderry, the London livery companies invested men and monies and laid out well-planned towns.

There is good music in Tyrone: allegorical songs, songs of maidens met in the mornings and of unfaithful wives.

The Strule (left and below)

From sweet Dungannon
* to Ballyshannon,*
from Cullyhanna
* to old Arboe,*
I've roved and rambled,
* caroused and gambled*
where songs did thunder
* and whiskey flow.*
It's light and airy
* I've tramped through Derry*
and to Portaferry
* in the County Down*
but in all my rakings
* and undertakings*
I met no equal
* to sweet Omagh town.*

Foothills of the Sperrins (opposite)

The Glenelly Valley (opposite)

Beautiful on a summer's morning as the clouds scud, these valleys can be quite different as the chill shadows creep out across their floors. Whilst your pace quickens, don't look back to see if nothing follows you from the dark bare hills.

Blessingbourne (above)

Elizabethan in its whimsy, the house always looks cheerful, mirrored in its neat round lake, but houses such as this are usually glimpsed only through thick rhododendrons, from the road.

101

Catherine's Lake, Baronscourt

Portrush harbour (opposite)

The
NORTH WEST

Bishop's Gate

The city's problem, apart from waverings between 'Derry' and 'Londonderry', has been that those who sited it here thought too well and too deeply. On a hill overlooking the wide Foyle river, it has always been considered by military men to have too great a strategic importance – real or symbolic – to leave to its citizens. Walk the walls from Bishop's Gate, by Double Bastion, Grand Parade and Nailer's Row, to Butcher's Gate and Magazine Street, to Coward's Bastion and Shipquay Gate, then by East Wall to Ferryquay Gate and back via Artillery Street to complete the circuit.

The indigenous population fought among themselves for a thousand years, Vikings came and went but Normans never took control, and once the walls were built the old lady pulled her skirts about her and was born again, unravaged, to keep her maidenhood through three long sieges. The city survived the 1641 rising. In 1649 she sided with Parliament and withstood the Royalists for twenty weeks but in December 1688 a handful of apprentice boys shut Ferryquay Gate on the heels of a departing garrison. With James II at the gates, the siege lasted 105 days and 7,000 died of starvation and disease. Rats were a shilling a head.

The Foyle and Waterside

The granting of the lands to the livery companies of London added the prefix of London to the old Derry. Some use it, many don't. The evocation of the siege left a city with tribal boundaries but a wondrous spirit. Catholic Bogside and Protestant Waterside unite in a fierce local pride.

City Walls

So, walk the walls and look down at the little hilly turning streets. Or walk the streets and glimpse the Foyle as you come down steep Shipquay Street from the Diamond, 'a diamond as big as a square'. Just as the people of a capital city have a character apart, so have those of a second city. Seek and ye shall find.

Out across the country the wind, sun and rain will be coming in from the west, from the Free State (the old name for the Republic of Ireland still favoured by people in the border counties), from the Atlantic, from the edge of the world. In the tiny roadways, cattle bundle and lurch in casual uneven herds blocking your car with their great heavy carpety brown-ness and black and white collies nip at their heels, making way for you as the farmer's second son looks impassively down from a high tractor's seat. The farmers are somewhere else, bales of hay and recalcitrant sheep on the back seat of their mud-spattered Mercedes. The first sons are at college learning law and courting doctors.

At unnamed crossroads, old ballrooms peel paint, the slipped neon no longer Mecca in a land gone to disco and Country 'n' Western.

The City of London did not find in Sir Thomas Phillips the man they wanted. But as in so many speculative ventures where the rewards appear attractive, few voiced the reservations which hovered in the scary recesses of their minds, and so Sir Thomas, after the forfeiture of the whole of Ulster in 1608, was engaged to supervise the plantation of the County of Londonderry. The Roe Valley went to the Haberdashers, Fishmongers and Skinners. The lands to the west of the Bann – in order, going south from the sea – to the Clothworkers, Merchant Tailors, Ironmongers, Mercers, Vintners and Salters. Goldsmiths and Grocers were on the banks of the Foyle. Phillips kept Limavady for himself. The Wardens and Commonality of the Mistery of the Fishmongers of the City of London planned *Balle Kelle* without the same sense of order seen in other Planters'

towns such as Moneymore and Draperstown.

Considerable capital was needed. A fortified bawn manned by old soldiers had to be built, and a Protestant church. Men were to be mustered twice a year and armed followers of the Irish chiefs to be dispatched to Connaught. Some of these did not take kindly to this scheme and carried on guerilla warfare from the woods, bogs and heights of Binevenagh, taking succour from other native Irish who had been offered little share of lands confiscated.

But those who had served the Crown in war fared little better and so were not inclined to defend the bawns. Some of the London 'undertakers' cut, sold and ran. A few kept the Irish as tenants, missing the point that ruthless expulsion was more 'efficient' in the long run.

The Model Farm, Ballykelly
Binevenagh (opposite)

Sampson's Tower, near Ballykelly

The seeds of a failed crop were everywhere. The land granted to the few Irish who got any was not enough to support the dispossessed. The old soldiers felt badly used by an ungrateful Crown. Landlords seeking a quick profit kept on Irish tenants rather than go to the expense of importing a loyal English and Scottish workforce. Who would not have exploited this recipe for chaos? And who to stop the rot, for few of the London men had any cognisance or appreciation of the scope of the scheme as Francis Bacon had outlined it. Few had the breadth of intellect to come to terms with a new land, an old culture and a great design. Meanwhile an Irish population, still much greater than was planned, smiled at their landlords. And waited.

To be fair to the Worshipful Companies, they had little heart in all this, and they saw the scheme for what it was, a tax on them to raise money for the Crown to pay for the settlement of the Irish question at the same time as they were being asked to put out even more money to carry out the work themselves.

Corruption and neglect were commonplace. Much of the timber from the great woods of the north-west, in theory cut down to build new towns and houses, was sold for quick profit. Commissioners of investigation came and went. Incompetence and embezzlement were discovered everywhere. The Irish, led by O'Cahans, O'Neills, MacDonnells and O'Donnells planned a rebellion. It would have succeeded, for the English had scarcely one hundred guns between them in a hostile land, but drink and bragging gave the rebels away.

108

Eventually the Crown acted. The City and the Irish Society were called to the Star Chamber, fined and made to forfeit their lands. But Parliament was later to reverse the judgement, setting City against Crown, sealing Charles's fate in the Civil War to come, and so Derry/Londonderry, for the first time, had a part in changing the history of the world. When the apprentice boys shut the gates almost forty years later, the city again set acts in motion which were to change the world. But first came the Great Rebellion of 1641 when the Irish rose, though failed to take the maiden city. The countryside was laid waste and thus a county which, had its timber-framed houses stood, might have looked much like rural Cheshire, is as we see it today.

But the street plans of the Planters are still with us and here and there, in and around the Plantation villages of a later and more peaceful century, the nineteenth, fine stone buildings provide a slightly more savoury legacy, though assisted emigration was still a feature of this age. Through all this, old beliefs, such as in the curative properties in certain wells, to be availed of by leaving votive mementos, persisted.

'Wart well', Dungiven

Though established and protected by Phillips, the architect of much of the preceding chaos, Limavady did not fare well either. Surviving the 1641 siege, it fell the next year. Built again, it was burnt again in 1689 whilst the men of the town defended Londonderry. The present layout and Georgian facades date from the early eighteenth-century builders. In 1851 Jane Ross noted down a tune played by a street fiddler here: 'The Londonderry Air', or 'Danny Boy'.

Limavady (left and below)
The river Roe (opposite)

There is an imperative which makes some men, and women, march. On 12 July the Orangemen march, and, for much the same reasons, members of the Royal Black Institution march in late August. On 15 August, Lady Day, Feast of the Assumption, a national holiday in many countries, the members of the Ancient Order of Hibernians march too. Their sashes are green, not orange, purple or black, but from a distance, a stranger unaware of the nuances which separate the twin cultures, might mistake one for the other. Banners, held high on polished wood poles, glint in the summer sun. Fife and drum step out on village streets. The red hand, symbol of the province, decorates all sashes.

The Ancient Order of Hibernians, Assumption Day, Draperstown (left and below)
Falls at Ness Country Park (opposite)

From Ulster's second city, the coast road runs north and east along the flatlands bordering Lough Foyle from where the tiny emigrant ships set sail in the 1770s. Beyond the long, fertile, reclaimed alluvial fields are the salt marsh, sand, mud and mussel beds of the Lough. At low tide the mud is dotted with oystercatcher, golden plover, dunlin, knot and curlew. In autumn, huge flocks of widgeon, 20,000 at a count, and brent geese browse on the eel grass. In winter, Bewick's and whooper swans cross the sea wall, and advance on the reclaimed land, taking some of it back to nature. In other winter fields, in the stubble, flickering fluttering flocks of tiny buntings, pippits and sparrows dodge between the short stalks. Stand still in the wind and watch high above, as the raptors – sparrow hawk, kestrel, merlin and peregrine – pick and dive on another supper before retreating to the dark of Ness Wood or the heights of Binevenagh.

The Foyle from Greysteel

At Mountsandel Fort, across the salmon-leap falls and 'The Cutts', were found the very first human traces in Ireland: flints, and the post-holes of huts, dating from the Middle Stone Age (Mesolithic). Beautiful Celtic gold brooches dating from 2 AD and Roman coins from the fifth century attest to the attractions of the 'fishy fruitful Bann' noted by Edmund Spenser, but the sand bar at the mouth of the river meant Coleraine lost out as a port to Portrush.

Frederick Augustus Hervey, Earl of Bristol, Bishop of Derry (1730–1803), modified this coast, and Europe, with his whims. His grand houses lie in ruins, but Bristol Hotels across the continent are witness to his patronage and profligacy. He had fat parsons race the soft sand to win a living, he built a temple to his cousin-mistress, Mrs Mussenden. He helped Catholic and Dissenter, and the spires of Ballyscullion, Bannagher and Tamlaghtfinlagan are his.

Drive east now, by Portstewart, to Portrush, the North's premier resort. Tall stucco houses catch the westering sun. Ramore Head heads proudly out to sea. John Rennie's harbour shelters sea-fishermen and long beaches dazzle. In the sandhills teenagers set out on rites of passage, golfers golf, old couples shelter. Each winter, the flower-patterned wallpaper on guesthouse walls awaits their return.

'The Cutts', near Coleraine

Downhill Strand and Mussenden Temple